THE
OCEAN

Exploring Our Blue Planet

MIRANDA KRESTOVNIKOFF

illustrated by
JILL CALDER

BLOOMSBURY
CHILDREN'S BOOKS
NEW YORK LONDON OXFORD NEW DELHI SYDNEY

For Amélie and Oliver,
who love the sea, above and below the waves —M. K.

For Tom, *who loves the sea, and Millie, Hatty, Annabelle,
and Molly, who swim in foreign seas* —J. C.

Contents

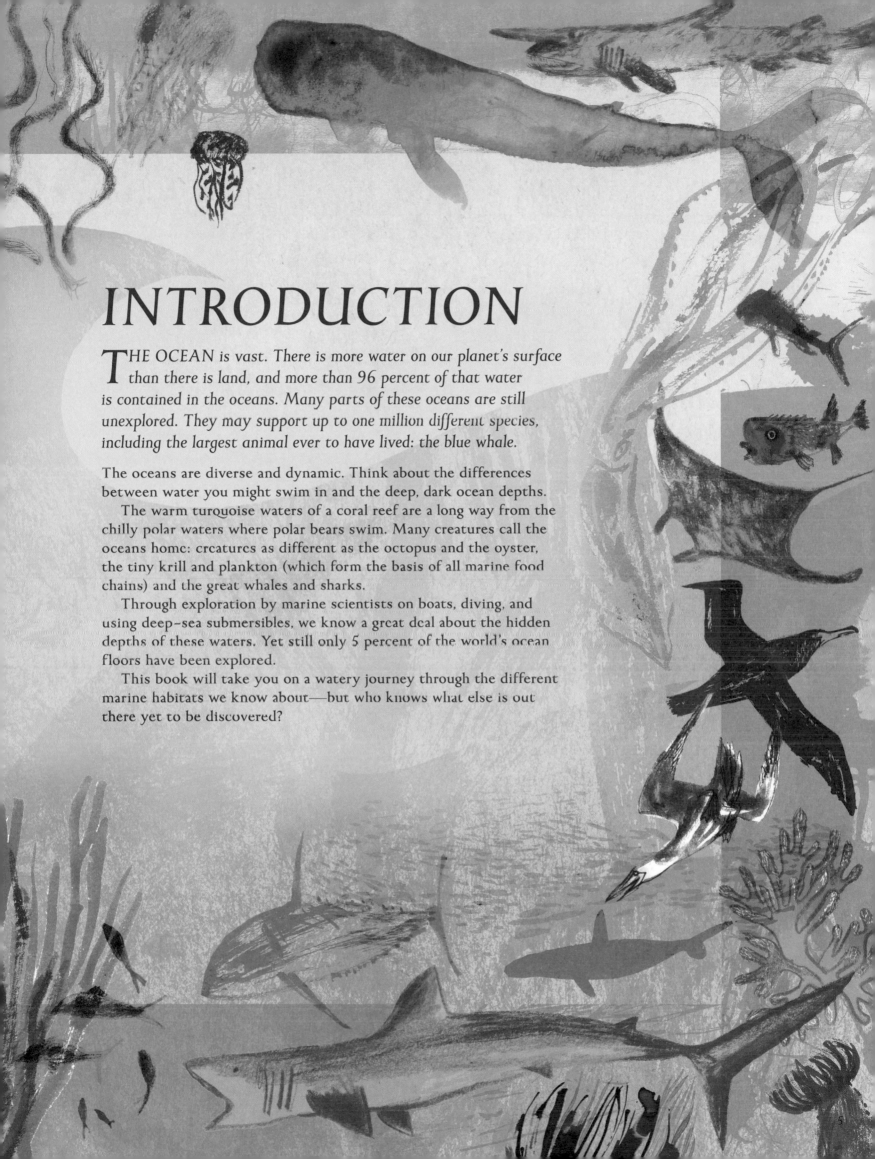

INTRODUCTION

THE OCEAN is vast. There is more water on our planet's surface than there is land, and more than 96 percent of that water is contained in the oceans. Many parts of these oceans are still unexplored. They may support up to one million different species, including the largest animal ever to have lived: the blue whale.

The oceans are diverse and dynamic. Think about the differences between water you might swim in and the deep, dark ocean depths.

The warm turquoise waters of a coral reef are a long way from the chilly polar waters where polar bears swim. Many creatures call the oceans home: creatures as different as the octopus and the oyster, the tiny krill and plankton (which form the basis of all marine food chains) and the great whales and sharks.

Through exploration by marine scientists on boats, diving, and using deep-sea submersibles, we know a great deal about the hidden depths of these waters. Yet still only 5 percent of the world's ocean floors have been explored.

This book will take you on a watery journey through the different marine habitats we know about—but who knows what else is out there yet to be discovered?

COASTLINES

COASTLINES are where most of us come into contact with the sea and are perhaps the first place where we encounter sea creatures, whether we are exploring tide pools or paddling in the shallows. The total length of the world's coastlines is almost impossible to measure. If you joined all the coastlines together, you would be able to circle the equator many times. You can find different animals depending on whether the area is made of rock, sand, or mud, and how high or low the tide moves. But coastal animals all have one thing in common: They are extremely hardy and adaptable.

Tide Pools

PROBABLY the most resilient animals in the ocean are those that make their homes in tide pools. They must be able to survive in extremely varied conditions. The pools warm up in the heat of the daytime sun but are flushed by cold water twice a day as the tide rushes in. They are pounded by the surf, and anything that can't hide is left exposed, to be dried out by the sun and buffeted by the wind.

Common limpet

Goby

Crabs

Wearing a suit of armor and waving a powerful pair of pincers is great protection. Many crabs also have a flattened body so they can crawl under rocks and into crevices. Crabs that live in tide pools tend to be fairly small and well camouflaged among the seaweed.

Starfish

These creatures look harmless but they are true carnivores (meat eaters) and prey on other tide pool creatures, such as mollusks. Starfish wrap themselves around their victims and grip with their tube feet to prise the two halves of their prey's shell apart. Then they turn their stomachs inside out and eat the soft parts of their prey. Incredibly, they are able to regrow their arms if one is damaged or lost!

Beadlet anemone

Starfish

Common shore crab

Blenny

Goby

Bladderwrack

Green
limpets

Anemones

Above water, beadlet anemones
look like bundles of jelly. They
stick to rocks and are closed
to protect themselves from
drying up. Their flower–like
tentacles extend when they are
submerged to sting their prey,
paralyze it, and bring it toward
their central mouth to eat.

Beadlet
anemone

Limpets

The limpet is well known for its
incredible ability to suck tightly onto a
rock so that predators cannot prise it off
and eat it. Once underwater, these mollusks
move around and graze on rock algae with
their tiny teeth. Just before the tide goes out,
they return to the exact same spot on the rock,
a circular shape known as a "home scar," where
the limpet's shell has ground against the rock.

Winkles

Tide pool fish

Some fish are able to crawl or wriggle out of the tide
pool if it becomes too warm and find refuge under
a damp rock. Clingfish have smooth scaleless skin that
enables them to squeeze into tiny spaces. They
also have a sucker on their bellies to cling onto
rocks. Gobies have eyes placed high on their
heads so they can identify predators from above.

Hermit crab

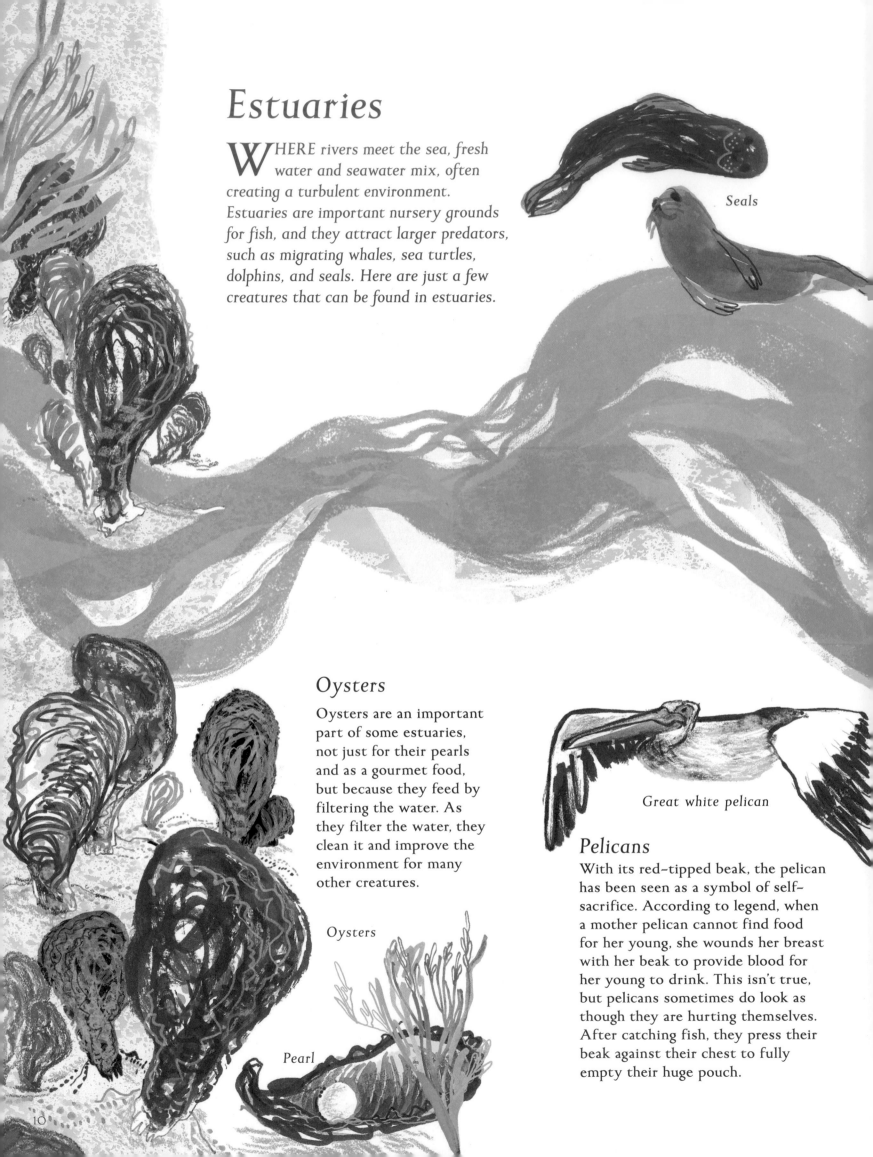

Estuaries

WHERE rivers meet the sea, fresh water and seawater mix, often creating a turbulent environment. Estuaries are important nursery grounds for fish, and they attract larger predators, such as migrating whales, sea turtles, dolphins, and seals. Here are just a few creatures that can be found in estuaries.

Seals

Oysters

Oysters are an important part of some estuaries, not just for their pearls and as a gourmet food, but because they feed by filtering the water. As they filter the water, they clean it and improve the environment for many other creatures.

Oysters

Pearl

Great white pelican

Pelicans

With its red-tipped beak, the pelican has been seen as a symbol of self-sacrifice. According to legend, when a mother pelican cannot find food for her young, she wounds her breast with her beak to provide blood for her young to drink. This isn't true, but pelicans sometimes do look as though they are hurting themselves. After catching fish, they press their beak against their chest to fully empty their huge pouch.

Porpoises and dolphins

Harbor porpoises sometimes swim up estuaries to prey on schooling fish. They are not as sociable as some of their other dolphin relatives, and instead they prefer to stay by themselves or in small groups. The word "porpoise" comes from the words for "pig" and "fish" in Latin, referring to either their snout or the noise they make, which sounds like a pig snort!

Spectacled porpoise

Harbor porpoise

La Plata dolphin

Australian pelican

Dalmatian pelican

Bird hide

Flying curlew

Black-headed gull

Salt Marshes

A salt marsh is grassland regularly inundated by saltwater at high tide, and it's bursting with life. You just have to look beneath the surface to find the humble worms, burrowing crabs, and shellfish that provide food for the tens of thousands of wading birds.

Bar-tailed godwits overwinter here on their migration from New Zealand to Alaska. The return journey, from Alaska to New Zealand, is the longest non-stop trip of any bird. Waders, like the curlew, godwits have evolved long, thin beaks so that they can find food in the deep mud.

   The salt marshes can be colorful places to live; they are blanketed by purple sea lavender in the summer and by red sea–blite in the autumn. Rare natterjack toads, with a yellow stripe down their backs, are one of the few amphibians that can tolerate seawater and make these marshes their home.

Natterjack toad

Bar-tailed godwit

Curlew

Fiddler crab

Mangrove Swamps

THE tropical equivalent of salt marshes, mangrove swamps are found in over one hundred countries worldwide. The word "mangrove" is a collective term for a group of shrubs or small trees that grow in tropical seawater.

Many different species of animal make their home among the salt-loving trees and shrubs with bizarre roots growing above the ground, because there is a constant food supply. Twigs and leaves from the mangrove trees provide food for crabs and are broken down into food for fish and shrimp when they fall in the water. The roots hide some unusual creatures, like the manatee and rare crocodiles.

Banded archerfish

Did you know that fish can spit? The banded archerfish forms a tube with its tongue against the roof of its mouth and can squirt a jet of water 2 to 3 yards. They try to hit prey resting on plants above the water, knocking them into the water where they can eat them. If that doesn't work, they can also leap out of the water to catch flying insects!

Crocodile or alligator?

Crocodiles and alligators occasionally live in the same place and, when they do, they are hard to tell apart. But there are differences. Alligators have a rounded snout whereas crocodiles have a more V-shaped head. Another difference is that when their jaws are closed, the fourth tooth of a crocodile sticks out. They feed on the abundance of fish and can remain hidden in the mangrove tree roots until they pounce on their prey.

Mangrove tree

Mangrove diamondback terrapin

Banded archerfish

Manatee

Crocodile

Sandy Coasts: Tropical Inhabitants

IT'S hard to make your home in a place that's always on the move—but sand can be a good place to hide and it's easy to dig a nest in. During the day, it can seem very quiet, but take a closer look: Just beneath the surface lie all sorts of creatures who burrow into the sand to escape from heat and predators, waiting for the tide to come in or nightfall to come before they emerge.

Horseshoe crabs

Horseshoe crabs

The horseshoe crab is actually an ancient relative of spiders. They look very strange, with blue blood and a spike-like tail. This spike is completely harmless and is used to flip the horseshoe crab the right way up if it is accidentally overturned. During the full moons of May and June, huge numbers of these ancient creatures gather on Delaware Beach. There are so many that the beach looks like a road paved with their shells. They gather to mate and lay eggs, which are important fuel for migrating birds.

Nesting turtles

In Costa Rica, thousands of olive ridley sea turtles arrive in the dead of night, haul their heart-shaped shells away from the safety of the water, and return to the beach where they hatched over a decade previously. This is known as an *arribada*. The large females dig a hole and lay a hundred or so eggs before returning to the water. Two months later, the sand will start to move as the new hatchlings emerge and scurry down the beach, dodging birds and crabs, to get to the safety of the sea.

Sand hoppers

If you move a piece of seaweed on a sandy beach, you will see a crowd of small jumping beasts. These are sand hoppers (also called beach hoppers) and, for their size, they have one of the biggest leaps of any animal.

Sand hoppers

Olive ridley sea turtle

Sandy Coasts: Temperate Inhabitants

Lugworm casts

Hidden creatures

As the tide goes out, it seems to take most sea life with it. But creatures hidden below the sand—like whelks, cockles, and razor clams—leave evidence of their lives in shells that are washed up for children to collect. Some of the owners of these protective shells are still there, though, hiding their soft bodies under the sand, away from the hungry gulls flying overhead. They lie in safety until the tide comes in again. The soft lugworm leaves a trace of where it is hiding: it produces a swirl or "cast" on the surface of the sand.

Lugworm

Bivalve mollusk

Cockle

Gulls

Hermit crab

Razor clam shell

Weever fish

Weever fish

Perfectly camouflaged, this small and deadly fish sits just beneath the surface of the sand. A terror to surfers and swimmers alike, the weever fish has venomous spines in its dorsal fin (a sharp fin on its back). The spines will pierce your skin if you step on it. Putting your foot into a bucket of hot water will help stop the pain—but it's better to watch your step!

Hermit crab

Occasionally, you will see a shell moving along the beach. Stolen shells from different creatures offer shelter and protection for hermit crabs. And when they outgrow their current shell, they will swap it for a new one, even battling another hermit crab to win a shell!

SHALLOW SEAS

SHALLOW seas are full of life. The diversity depends only on whether the seabed is rocky or sandy. Sand is shifting all the time, so creatures must be able to cope with being constantly on the move. In contrast, on a rocky seabed there is something solid to make your home on. This is where you find huge forests of kelp, gardens of floating seaweeds, and coral reefs in a huge variety of colors.

Rocky Seabeds

ROCK provides a solid base to hold on to while surviving the rip and roar of currents and tides. Under the water's surface, there is a hidden garden of floating fronds with names like maidenhair and peacock's tail. There are seaweeds and organisms like algae, which have a holdfast or clamp that anchors the fronds to the rock and enables them to survive the push and pull of the waves. Seaweeds come in three main color groups: greens, browns, and reds.

Glass anemone

Green

Green seaweeds, like the land plants they are related to, need the most sunlight and are found in the shallowest water.

Brown

There are many different shades of brown seaweeds. They are generally tough and slippery and found in deeper water, as they are able to survive with less sunlight. Some of them have gas-filled bladders that float, lifting the fronds off the seabed close to the surface and creating a seaweed garden that is a valuable nursery for young fish.

Peacock's tail seaweed

Limpets

Bladderwrack

Ballan wrasse

Sea spaghetti

Red

Red seaweeds are able to grow in much deeper water—even as deep as 100 yards. Little light penetrates this far into the ocean, but they can survive even in very low light levels.

Uses

Seaweed is used by a huge variety of animals, and not just as food. Fish, like the corkwing wrasse and ballan wrasse, use it to make nests. They carefully select pieces of seaweed of a certain length or thickness. The males guard their nests fiercely—even fighting off human divers to defend them.

Beadlet anemone

Starfish

Plumose anemone

Corkwing wrasse

Maidenhair seaweed

Kelp Forests

KELP forests are just as important to the environment as rainforests on land and support just as varied a number of species. Kelp is an algae, and giant kelp is the biggest algae in the world—it can grow up to 2 feet per day, eventually reaching more than 100 feet tall. Like a tree, it has a long stem with many leaf-like fronds at the top and, just like a rainforest, a kelp forest has a top canopy layer with other layers beneath, each with its own distinct group of animals and plants.

Sea otters in kelp eating sea urchins

Shrimp

Fronds
On the seabed, where the enormous fronds of kelp attach to rocks, there is a network of nooks and crannies for small animals such as worms and crustaceans to burrow. The kelp's stem ("stipe") provides a place for seaweeds and grazing animals, such as urchins and limpets, to live. The huge fronds can be coated in a slime to stop them from being grazed, but they are often covered in a range of animals (sponges and sea mats) and red seaweeds.

Sea urchins
Related to the starfish, sea urchins have a hard, round shell called a "test" and are covered in purple spines. They move using their tube feet, which have suckers on them. The purple sea urchin feeds on giant kelp. If the sea urchin numbers get out of control, they can eat through the kelp holdfasts, causing them to drift off and die, and damaging or destroying vast parts of the kelp forest.

Sea otters

Often seen wrapped up in sea kelp, sea otters use the long fronds as a safety net to stop them drifting away while they sleep. Otters have the densest fur of any mammal, with hairs so tightly packed that the water never gets through to their skin. They are extremely well adapted to a life at sea; they can lift and turn over rocks to find food that they catch with their forepaws. They have a pouch of skin in which they store their food and a favorite stone! At the surface, otters feed by smashing crabs and sea urchins open using this stone.

A balancing act

Like any ecosystem, the food chain must be balanced to have a diversity of species. Sea otters are a classic example of a "keystone species." This means that they are hugely important to keep the ecosystem in balance. They feed on sea urchins. But years ago, when sea otters were hunted for their dense pelts, the number of sea urchins got so large that they ate away at the kelp, and the forests dwindled.

Kelp

Sea otter

Sea urchin

Brittle star

Coral Reefs

BUSTLING. *Colorful. Vibrant. Coral reefs are incredibly busy and are some of the most important and beautiful habitats on the planet. Their humble architects are tiny marine organisms called coral. If you look at a coral closely, it is made up of thousands of identical creatures called polyps (related to jellyfish and anemones) that together form a coral colony. For most reefs, the tiny polyps create hard external skeletons which over time form coral reefs. Most corals also rely on the algae that live inside their tissues and need sunlight and warm water to thrive. This is why coral reefs are only found in shallow water, where plenty of sun reaches the sea floor. Corals feed by extending their tentacles to catch plankton in the surrounding water currents.*

Bumphead parrotfish

Parrotfish

This fish's front teeth are fused together to form a "beak," which it uses to rip off chunks of coral from the reef and grind them down to extract the algae inside. Incredibly, these fish are able to change from male to female and back again throughout their life!

Plate coral

Spanish dancer

The Great Barrier Reef

As the largest living structure on the planet, the Great Barrier Reef is mind-blowing in terms of its size and diversity. Stretching 1,400 miles and covering an area roughly the size of Italy, this natural icon can be seen from outer space. Around 8 percent of the world's total fish species can be found just within the Great Barrier Reef.

Giant clams

The largest specimens of giant clams recorded have been over 4 feet across! Giant clams are a "bivalve," which literally means "two leaves of a door," referring to its two shells which, in some of the larger clams, can't actually close tightly.

Sea snakes

Sea snakes live their whole lives in the ocean but must surface every hour or so to breathe. Many can't survive on land because they don't have special scales (scutes) on their bellies to grip with, like land snakes. When they go underwater, they breathe through their nostrils (which are really high up on their head). They can also breathe through their skin. They have just one lung, which is almost as long as their body.

Nudibranchs

A nudibranch is like a sea snail without a shell. These creatures rely on their bright colors and sometimes toxic chemicals to defend themselves. They often eat dangerous creatures and then adopt the poisons in their own defense. One of the most stunning to watch is the Spanish dancer, which moves, as its name suggests, like a Spanish flamenco dancer. The adults are often red with white feathery gills. They lay eggs in a delicate, coiled ribbon called a sea rose, which is laced with toxins to deter predators.

Pufferfish

Pufferfish can expand quickly when disturbed to several times their normal size. Almost all pufferfish contain a toxin that makes them taste horrible and is deadly to other fish and humans.

Banded sea krait

Pufferfish

Branch coral

Giant clam

Brain coral

Freckled porcupinefish

Parrotfish

Garden eels

Sandy Seabeds

SAND is constantly shifting, which means that very little sea life stays still for long. Large animals roam the seabed in search of food, while smaller fish and invertebrates hide among the grains. Some of the creatures that live on a sand seabed are quite extraordinary . . .

Garden eels

Swimming over a sandy seabed, divers often think they can see grass in the distance which seems to disappear as they get closer. But this isn't grass—it's a colony of garden eels reacting to the threat of an approaching predator. These small, thin eels spend their entire adult life with their tails tucked into the sand and their heads swaying to and fro in the current. They create a solid wall for their burrow by using mucus to stick the sand grains together.

Sea mouse

This strange-looking creature is actually a segmented (made of lots of similar parts) worm, but from the top it looks quite hairy. It spends most of its life hiding in the sand and has stunning iridescent hairs along its back, which reflect the light in many different colors.

Sea mouse

Scallops

Scallops

Not only are scallops good to eat,
but they also have a funny way of
swimming—they clap their shells
quickly, which moves a jet of water
past the shell hinge and pushes the
scallop forward.

Stingray

Stingrays

Stingrays are a popular tourist attraction and are surprisingly
friendly, despite their name. These gentle fish, with a
skeleton made of cartilage, are lured in to the coast by the
promise of discarded fish from the local fishermen's catch.

Manatee

Seagrass Beds

SEAGRASS *looks like its name: meadows of green grass-like fronds that grow in shallow, warm, sunlit water on a sandy seabed. They are the only true flowering marine plants, and they provide food and shelter for hundreds of species.*

Manatee

Manatees are some of the gentlest and most mysterious creatures in the ocean. They communicate with squeaks and chirps and are enormous aquatic mammals that can weigh over 1,000 pounds and feed mostly on vegetation, eating about 10 percent of their body mass every day. Manatee calves suckle from teats in their mother's armpits! Slow-moving, they are related to elephants, and the scars on their backs tell the story of all too frequent encounters with boat propellers, as they are often unable to swim quickly enough to get out of the way.

Seahorses

These magical creatures swim upright and have a tiny fin on their back which moves them along. However, they spend much of their time with their tail coiled around a piece of coral or seagrass, using their long noses to suck up plankton. Seahorses are the only animals on the planet where the male gives birth. After an elaborate and graceful courtship, the female transfers her eggs into the male's pouch, where they are fertilized. The male holds them there until they are ready to hatch, releasing tiny (but fully formed) seahorses into the water.

Seahorse

Seagrass

Shipwrecks

OUR seas are littered with roughly three million wrecks from our rich, ten thousand–year maritime history—but what happens to a ship when it sinks? Sunken ships, planes, and submarines create artificial reefs and a new habitat for marine life. They are exciting places for divers to explore and for marine life to call home. Once a ship has hit the seabed, organisms such as the spores of seaweed, the eggs and larvae of fish, anemones, and corals will settle on its solid structure. Over many years, nature will take over the human-made wreck.

HMS Scylla

In March 2004, the *HMS Scylla* was purposefully sunk in the English Channel to create an interesting and safe place for divers to explore. Within a month, tube worms, barnacles, and spider crabs had colonized the nooks and crannies of the 2,700-ton frigate. Within a year, over fifty species had been recorded on the *Scylla* and, after less than two years, ocean life had smothered 80 percent of the wreck, including corkwing wrasse, queen scallops, and pink sea fans. Sinking a ship like this has taught us a huge amount about how marine life eventually balances itself out in a new environment.

Goggle-eye fish

Great barracuda

SS Thistlegorm

In 1941, the *SS Thistlegorm*, a British armed Merchant Navy ship, sank in the Red Sea. It is now one of the top ten diving sites in the world. Divers exploring the wreck can still see the machine guns, trucks, motorbikes, and other military supplies it was carrying. But, over time, nature has softened this wartime vessel, covering it with corals and algae and creating a safe haven for many species of marine life, including barracuda, batfish, lionfish, and sea turtles.

Black
damselfish

Barracuda
school

Orbicular
batfish

31

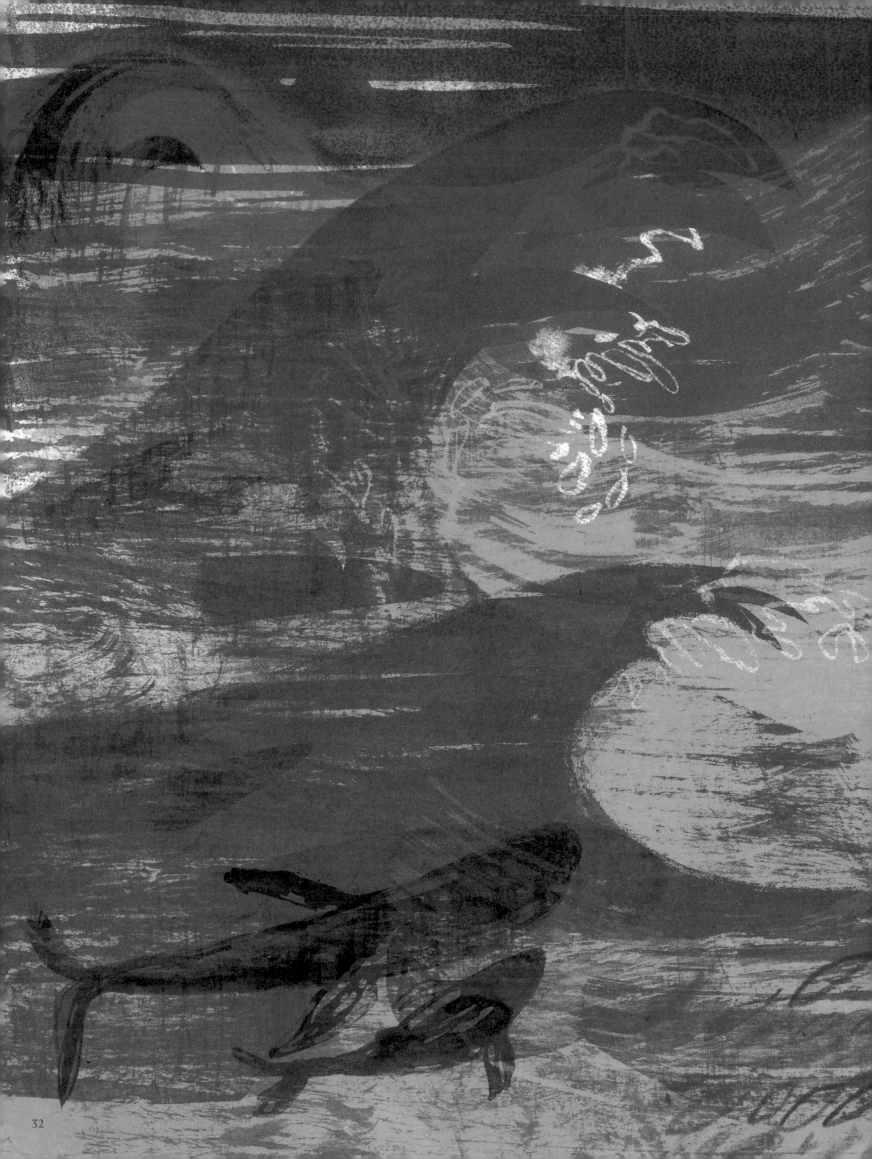

THE OPEN OCEAN

OCEANS are vast wildernesses that humans have barely explored. Huge animals dwell in their depths, and there may still be many mysterious creatures which we have not yet discovered. In the open ocean, most life is found in the top 700 feet of the water, as this is the area which is richest in nutrients. The types of creatures found in different oceans depend on the temperature and the saltiness of the water.

Whales and Dolphins

WHALES, dolphins, and porpoises are closely related animals in the cetacean family. They are air-breathing mammals, like us, and live in social groups. There are around ninety different species, from the tiny, 4-foot-long vaquita to the majestic blue whale (measuring an impressive 80 feet in length or more). Other members of this charismatic family include the orca or killer whale (really a dolphin), the Arctic narwhal, and the strange and rare river dolphins of China and the Amazon.

Working together

Various different groups of dolphins around the world have adapted different methods to work together—in Laguna, dolphins herd fish into the shallows on the beach and even work with the local fishermen to catch the fish so that both can benefit from the bounty. Other groups or "pods" work together to herd shoals of fish into a huge ball by whistling directions to each other and even stunning the fish by producing loud noises to confuse them. They are also one of the few animals that use tools—dolphins in Australia have been seen putting sponges on their beaks to protect themselves when hunting among sharp rocks and coral.

Bottlenose dolphins

Bottlenose dolphins live in big groups and are very intelligent. Although we don't fully understand their language, it seems they have unique whistles for their names and can be taught to recognize human words and even sentences. Bottlenose dolphins are incredibly playful creatures and are one of the few animals that will actively seek out the company of humans and try to interact with them.

Vaquita

Humpback whale

Blue whale

Narwhal

Sperm whale

Orca

Bait ball
of fish

Spotted
dolphin

White-sided
dolphin

Bottlenose dolphin

Ocean Giants

THE largest creatures on the planet lurk in our oceans, with their huge mass supported by the water around them. Here, they can maximize on the almost limitless supply of food, moving from one place to another to gorge on seasonal abundances of fish and plankton.

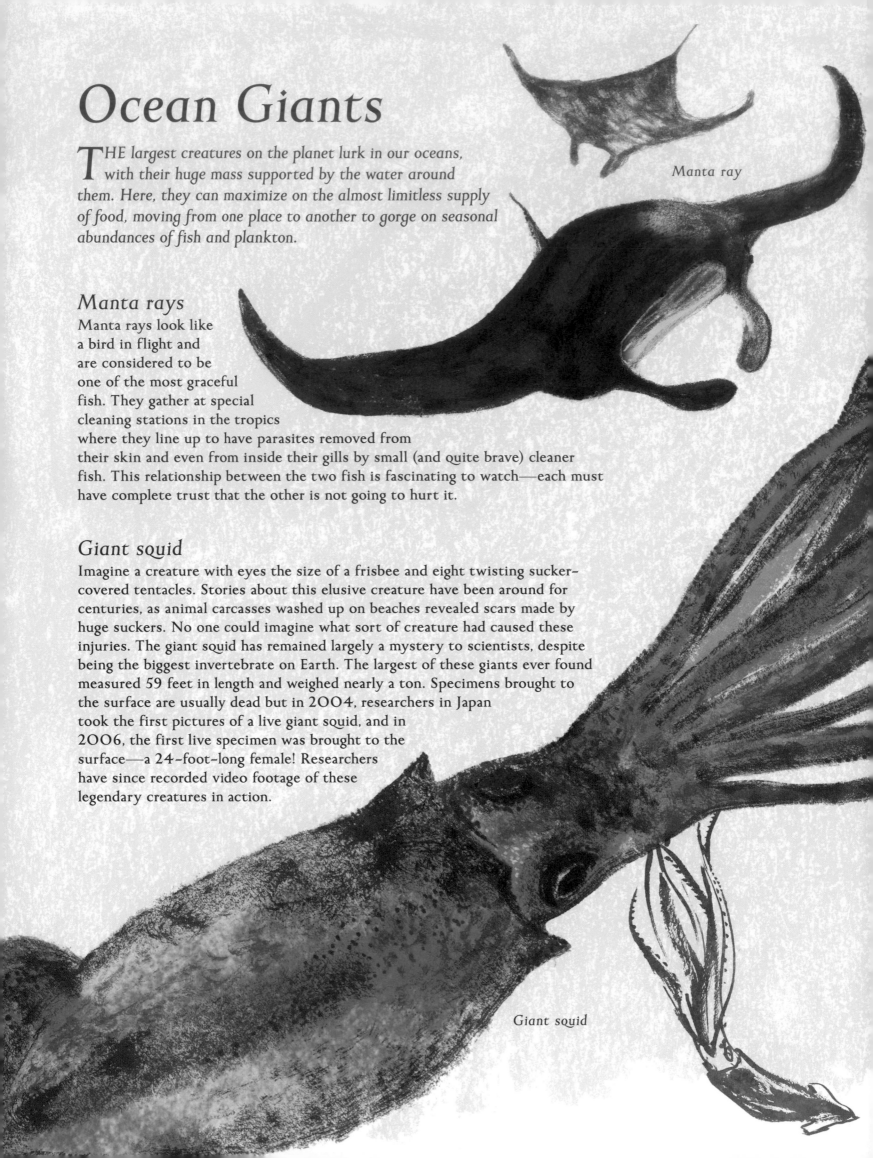

Manta ray

Manta rays

Manta rays look like a bird in flight and are considered to be one of the most graceful fish. They gather at special cleaning stations in the tropics where they line up to have parasites removed from their skin and even from inside their gills by small (and quite brave) cleaner fish. This relationship between the two fish is fascinating to watch—each must have complete trust that the other is not going to hurt it.

Giant squid

Imagine a creature with eyes the size of a frisbee and eight twisting sucker-covered tentacles. Stories about this elusive creature have been around for centuries, as animal carcasses washed up on beaches revealed scars made by huge suckers. No one could imagine what sort of creature had caused these injuries. The giant squid has remained largely a mystery to scientists, despite being the biggest invertebrate on Earth. The largest of these giants ever found measured 59 feet in length and weighed nearly a ton. Specimens brought to the surface are usually dead but in 2004, researchers in Japan took the first pictures of a live giant squid, and in 2006, the first live specimen was brought to the surface—a 24-foot-long female! Researchers have since recorded video footage of these legendary creatures in action.

Giant squid

Ocean sunfish

Ocean sunfish
This is the heaviest known bony fish in the world. It has no scales, and, instead of swimming like a normal fish does, it prefers to lie on its side, often at the water's surface—either to bask in the warmth of the sun (hence its name) or possibly to allow seabirds to pick parasites off its skin.

Manta ray

Moon jellyfish

Leatherback
turtle

Gray whale

Ocean Travelers

MANY creatures in the open ocean are travelers migrating hundreds, if not thousands, of miles to find food and a mate. It is still a mystery how so many species navigate such vast distances, but we know that some are guided by ocean currents and temperatures.

Leatherback turtle

The leatherback turtle is massive: it is the largest, heaviest, longest-living, and most wide-ranging of all the world's turtle species. These giants can weigh as much as a cow and reach about 7 feet in length! They cruise the open oceans in search of their favorite food, jellyfish. Their throats have dozens of spines, which face backwards to stop the jellyfish escaping as they are swallowed.

Gray whales

Most whales travel to cold water for food and to warmer water to give birth. In 2015, a gray whale was reported migrating all the way from Russia to Mexico and back again, a total of nearly 14,000 miles in only 172 days! Incredibly, researchers have found that whales often don't return on the same route. This means that they must memorize their journey rather than just following the coastline.

Blue whale

Bluefin tuna

Tuna

Tuna are incredible travelers because of the speeds they can reach—up to 45 miles per hour. To reach these sorts of speeds, they raise their body temperature, which warms their blood and enables them to swim faster and to survive in colder water.

Long-finned pilot whales

Pilot whales are actually a type of dolphin and can live in groups of several hundred individuals. The whales make many different kinds of sounds to communicate: squeaks, whistles, buzzes, and rapid clicks that they use in echolocation. Echolocation is the use of sound waves and their echoes to "see" underwater: sound waves hit an object and produce echoes, which are converted by the animal's brain into an image of the surrounding environment.

Sardines

The sardine run of southern Africa is a huge migration. Billions of sardines spawn in the cool water near the tip of South Africa. Sardines group together for protection and the shoals are vast, often more than 4 miles long and nearly 100 feet deep. The sardine run is clearly visible from the air, and this bounty of food creates a feeding frenzy along the coastline. Predators gather to feed, including sharks, fur seals, and common dolphins (who specialize in rounding up the fish into huge bait balls of 30 to 60 feet in diameter).

Sardines

Long-finned
pilot whale

Seabirds

MOST birds we see from day to day make their homes on land, but there are vast numbers that roam the waters of the world's oceans. Some species spend most of the year at sea, only coming to land when they need to breed. These birds are well adapted to cope with salt water and have ingenious ways to hunt down their food.

Puffin

Puffin

Beating their wings 400 times a minute, puffins need this speed because they are under constant attack from aerial predators, like the black-backed gull.

Underwater, they are superb swimmers and they feed on sand eels, using a serrated (jagged) tongue to hold one fish in their beaks while they catch another one.

Great frigatebird

The males of this species have a flamboyant red throat pouch, which they inflate to impress females. Masters of gliding flight, these birds have a massive wingspan and slender bodies. They are also keen thieves, carefully watching other birds as they fly and chasing them to make them give up their food.

Gannet

A gannet can plummet from heights of 100 feet, hitting the water at speeds of up to 60 miles per hour, to seize its prey with pinpoint precision. Over time, their heads have evolved to contain a special cushioning to protect their brains from the impact when they hit the water.

Female frigatebird

Nesting male frigatebird

Gannets

Sharks

CRUISING the open ocean are more than four hundred different types of sharks. Lots of people think that sharks are ruthless killers, but very few shark species have ever attacked humans and scientists think that most attacks are a case of mistaken identity. Sharks live in temperate and tropical waters and many perform long migrations.

Sharks can pick up tiny electromagnetic pulses from other living creatures through special jelly-filled sensory organs in their heads called ampullae of Lorenzini. These are so sensitive, they can sense a heart beating from several miles away!

To survive, sharks need to move water over their gills to absorb oxygen. To do this, they can either swim continuously through the water to ventilate their gills, or remain still and pump water over them.

Whale shark

The whale shark is the largest fish in the sea. It can grow to be 40 feet long and weigh up to 25 tons. Their mouths are large enough to fit a human inside!

Tiger shark

The tiger shark is known as the garbage can of the ocean and is famous for devouring anything it comes across. They have been found with car licence plates, tires, and even a fur coat in their stomachs!

Dwarf lanternshark

The smallest shark, the dwarf lanternshark can fit into a human hand. They are able to produce bioluminescence (light) to trick and trap their prey.

Hammerhead shark

Blue shark

Blue sharks migrate across entire oceans throughout their lives. They are excellent swimmers and the only shark that is blue.

The bizarre cookiecutter shark is only around 20 inches long, but the wounds it creates can be very damaging. It latches onto its prey and then twists and cuts with its teeth to form a neat, circular hole. Wounds like this have been found on dolphins, whales, seals, and even other sharks.

Cookiecutter shark

The fastest shark is the shortfin mako shark, which can reach speeds of around 50 miles per hour.

Shortfin mako shark

Fish Shoal

Greenland sharks can grow up to 23 feet in length and are found swimming slowly through the cold, deep waters of the North Atlantic. Recently one female was estimated to be nearly 400 years old—a record for any vertebrate!

Greenland shark

Mermaid's purses

Blacktip reef shark

Megamouth shark

Most sharks give birth to live babies, but some species lay eggs. These can be seen washed up on the beach in "mermaid's purses." The "purse" is a protective egg case with tendrils that attach it to something solid, such as a coral or piece of seaweed, while the baby shark develops inside.

Angel shark

The megamouth shark is the rarest and most mysterious shark species. It was discovered in 1976, and there have been only about sixty sightings of it since.

The Blue Whale

THE blue whale is the largest animal to have ever lived on our planet. It can reach the length of a Boeing 737 plane. Far bigger than any of the dinosaurs, these whales are supported by the seawater—on land they would simply collapse.

Blue whales are some of the rarest animals on Earth as they were hunted by whalers in the 1900s for the oil in their blubber. Only 10,000 to 25,000 blue whales are believed to still swim the world's oceans, and they are now a protected species.

Strangely, for such a huge creature, they feed on some of the smallest creatures in the sea: krill. A blue whale can consume several tons of these tiny shrimp-like creatures every day.

There are very few animals that could prey upon a blue whale, but sharks and killer whales have been known to attack them and, sadly, many are injured or die each year when they are hit by large ships.

These gentle giants are found in all of our oceans and usually swim alone or in pairs, spending their summers feeding in polar waters and migrating huge distances toward the equator as winter arrives.

THE POLAR SEAS

AT the top and the bottom of the planet lie the North and South Poles. The chilly polar seas that surround them are full of silent, drifting icebergs and sheets of creaking ice. In the warmer months, much of the ice melts. So much water is held as ice at the poles that if all the world's ice melted, the oceans would rise about 230 feet. Because of the nutrients in the ice, life thrives in the sea directly around, and under, the ice. The Arctic Ocean (in the north) and the Southern Ocean (by Antarctica) are linked by their cold climate, but the types of wildlife that live in each ocean are very different. Life at both poles is harsh and extreme, which means that the animals who live there are mostly large and often dangerous.

Polar Bears

THE Arctic Ocean is the world's smallest ocean. The average thickness of the Arctic ice is around 6 to 9 feet, although there are some areas as thick as 65 feet or more. Holes in the ice are vital so that marine mammals, like seals and walruses, can breathe.

In the northern Arctic, the frozen water is home to the world's largest carnivore: the polar bear. Polar bears are incredible swimmers and they are experts at sniffing out seals. Polar bears can smell seals on the ice from 20 miles away and even detect their movements under more than three feet of ice. They have transparent fur (which looks white) and black skin underneath, which absorbs heat from the sun. They hibernate in dens during the winter. They are perfectly adapted for life in such a harsh environment.

Female bears give birth to twin cubs in their snow dens in November or December. Each cub is born the size of a guinea pig. They stay in the safety of the den for up to five months and then follow their mother for the next two years, learning all the skills and survival techniques they need for life on the ice.

Arctic Creatures

EXTREME cold, extreme seasonal changes in daylight, and extreme winds make life here really tough, but the Arctic is actually teeming with wildlife that has adapted to these harsh conditions over many thousands of years, all of it highly specialized and equipped with ways of withstanding this harsh environment.

Narwhals

Narwhal

One of the most extraordinary animals found in the Arctic water is the narwhal. These bizarre-looking creatures are members of the dolphin family. The males have twisted tusks that can grow up to 9 feet long. These tusks are, in fact, the extended left canine tooth, which grows through their upper lip. These tusks have up to ten million nerve endings and what narwhals use them for is not really known. Some scientists think they might be used to fight other males for females, but this is not certain.

Walrus

With their long tusks, walruses are powerful predators, with males weighing up to 3,700 pounds. Unlike other Arctic mammals, they are almost completely hairless, so they rely on a thick layer of blubber for insulation against the sub-zero temperatures of the Arctic water. Their funny-looking whiskers are used to find their food, mostly shellfish, by touch rather than by sight.

Ribbon seal

Walrus

Polar bear

Beluga whales

Whales

Many species of whale live in the Arctic water, including the ghostly-colored beluga whale. The beluga is camouflaged white for protection against predators such as the polar bear and orca. Belugas are strange-looking whales: they have no dorsal fin and a very large forehead, due to a large lump of fatty tissue called the "melon" that they use in echolocation. Their calls are extremely high-pitched, and because of this they are sometimes called "the canary of the sea!"

Seals

Ungainly on land, seals are unbelievably graceful under water and live in oceans all over the world. In the Arctic, seals are a favorite snack for polar bears and are hunted through holes in the ice. Seal pups are born on the ice and here they are most at risk, especially if their parents are away hunting for fish. The majority of the world's seal population actually lives in Antarctica, where they are able to survive because they have no natural land predators, unlike their northern counterparts.

Harp seal pup

Harp seal

South polar skua

Antarctic Creatures

ANTARCTICA is the coldest place on Earth, so you would imagine that it is pretty inhospitable to life. However, sea life is plentiful, and it supports huge populations of land animals—vast colonies of penguins and plenty of predators who lie in wait for them.

Penguins

How has a bird that can't fly managed to be so successful? In Antarctica, penguin colonies contain hundreds of thousands, even millions of birds—bigger than many of the world's cities! They are able to survive because they have few predators. There are seventeen species of penguins in the world but only seven are found in Antarctica, including the largest—the emperor penguin.

Although they can't fly, they are superb swimmers, and emperor penguins can hold their breath for 20 minutes. Under the water, they need to keep alert to avoid leopard seals and killer whales, and on land, chicks and eggs are in danger of becoming prey to the skua seabird. Penguins have an outer layer of oily, waterproof feathers, which cover soft down feathers, and under that a thick layer of fat, all of which protect them against the harsh, year-round cold.

Emperor penguin

Penguin chick

Wandering
albatross

Nesting
albatross

Albatross

With a wingspan of up to 11 feet, the largest of any
bird, albatrosses are able to soar to save energy,
meaning they can fly for days, even weeks, without
landing. They return every two years to the same spot
and the same mate to breed and lay their single egg.

Elephant seals

Elephant seals are the largest seal species and the
males have a strange, long nose to match their name.
You wouldn't want to get too close to them as
they smell really bad and could squash you
with their immense body weight.
Males engage in fearsome battles,
crashing their massive 4-ton
bodies against each other.

Elephant seal

Krill

One of the most important creatures in the Southern Ocean is one of
the smallest: at around 2 inches long, these small, shrimp-like creatures
are the fuel that runs the engine of the Earth's marine ecosystems.
Without krill, most of the life forms in Antarctica would disappear. Pink
and opaque, Antarctic krill gather in huge shoals which at certain times
of the year can be seen from space. Krill eat phytoplankton (tiny,
single-celled plants that drift near the ocean's surface) but they
themselves are eaten by a large number of creatures: whales,
seals, penguins, squid, and fish.

Phytoplankton

Krill

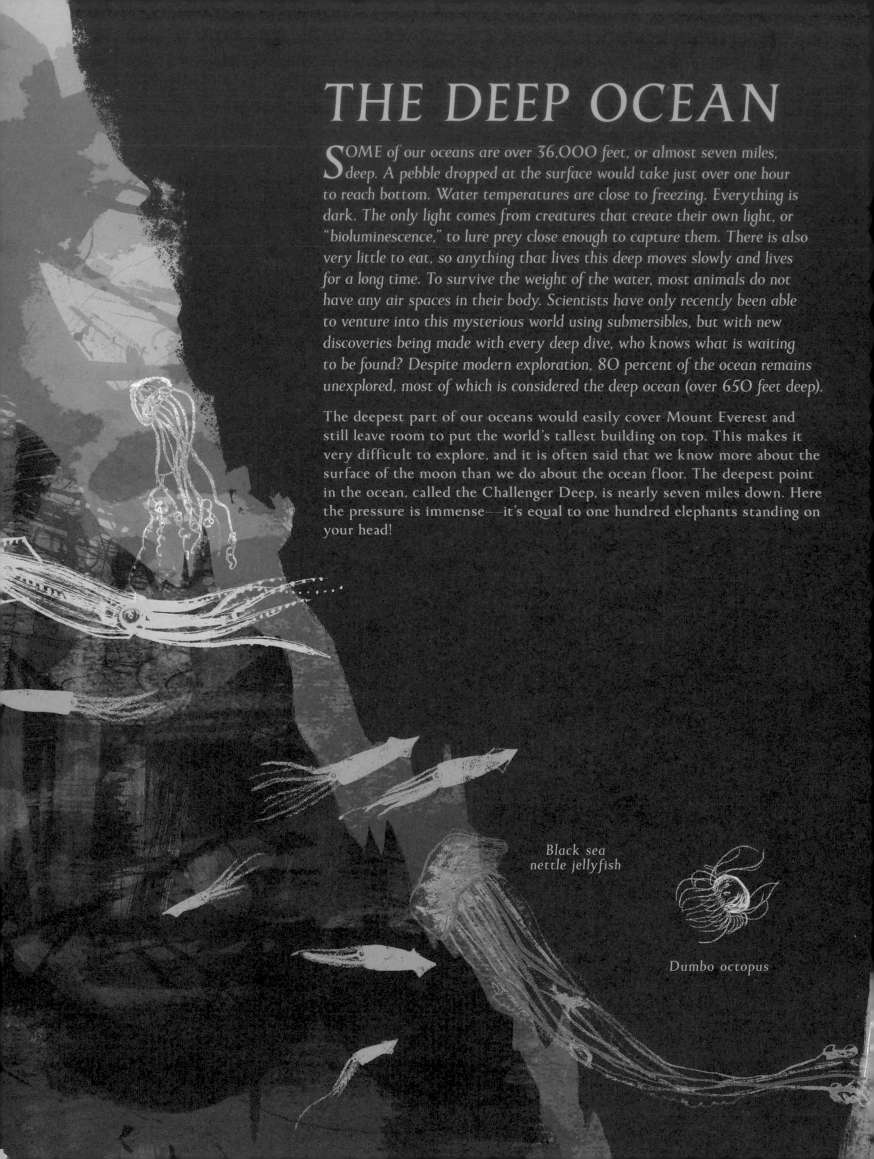

THE DEEP OCEAN

SOME of our oceans are over 36,000 feet, or almost seven miles, deep. A pebble dropped at the surface would take just over one hour to reach bottom. Water temperatures are close to freezing. Everything is dark. The only light comes from creatures that create their own light, or "bioluminescence," to lure prey close enough to capture them. There is also very little to eat, so anything that lives this deep moves slowly and lives for a long time. To survive the weight of the water, most animals do not have any air spaces in their body. Scientists have only recently been able to venture into this mysterious world using submersibles, but with new discoveries being made with every deep dive, who knows what is waiting to be found? Despite modern exploration, 80 percent of the ocean remains unexplored, most of which is considered the deep ocean (over 650 feet deep).

The deepest part of our oceans would easily cover Mount Everest and still leave room to put the world's tallest building on top. This makes it very difficult to explore, and it is often said that we know more about the surface of the moon than we do about the ocean floor. The deepest point in the ocean, called the Challenger Deep, is nearly seven miles down. Here the pressure is immense—it's equal to one hundred elephants standing on your head!

Black sea
nettle jellyfish

Dumbo octopus

Ocean trench walls

Nautile deep-sea submersible

Ocean pinnacle

Luminous squid

Humboldt squid

Hydrothermal Vents

THERE was a time when scientists believed that no life in the sea could survive without sunlight. Then they made a submersible expedition near the Galapagos in 1977. Scientists discovered an unexpected community of life around structures named "hydrothermal vents." This was a new kind of ecosystem flourishing in the dark and all based around a toxic gas. Scientists had never imagined that such a thing could exist! Many scientists now think that life on Earth could have begun at vents like these, over three billion years ago.

Tube worms

Tube worms

One of the most intriguing new species found by scientists is a giant tube worm: it can grow up to 8 feet tall in two years! What puzzles scientists about these worms is that they don't seem to have any way of feeding—no mouth and no digestive system!

Eelpout

White crab

White starfish

Eruption

Hydrothermal vents are similar to hot springs on land: deep down on the ocean floor, the water seeps into the ocean bed where it is heated by super-hot magma and it dissolves minerals from the rock around it. It then erupts at high pressure, and the mix of hot water and minerals supports a unique community of animals not found anywhere else on the planet. Many of the creatures are white—they don't need to be colored, as there is no light to see with.

Ghostly creatures

Other creatures found here are: eyeless shrimp (which have heat detecting spots on their heads), eelpouts (big-lipped fish), and large colonies of ghostly-looking white crabs which feast on other creatures' leftovers.

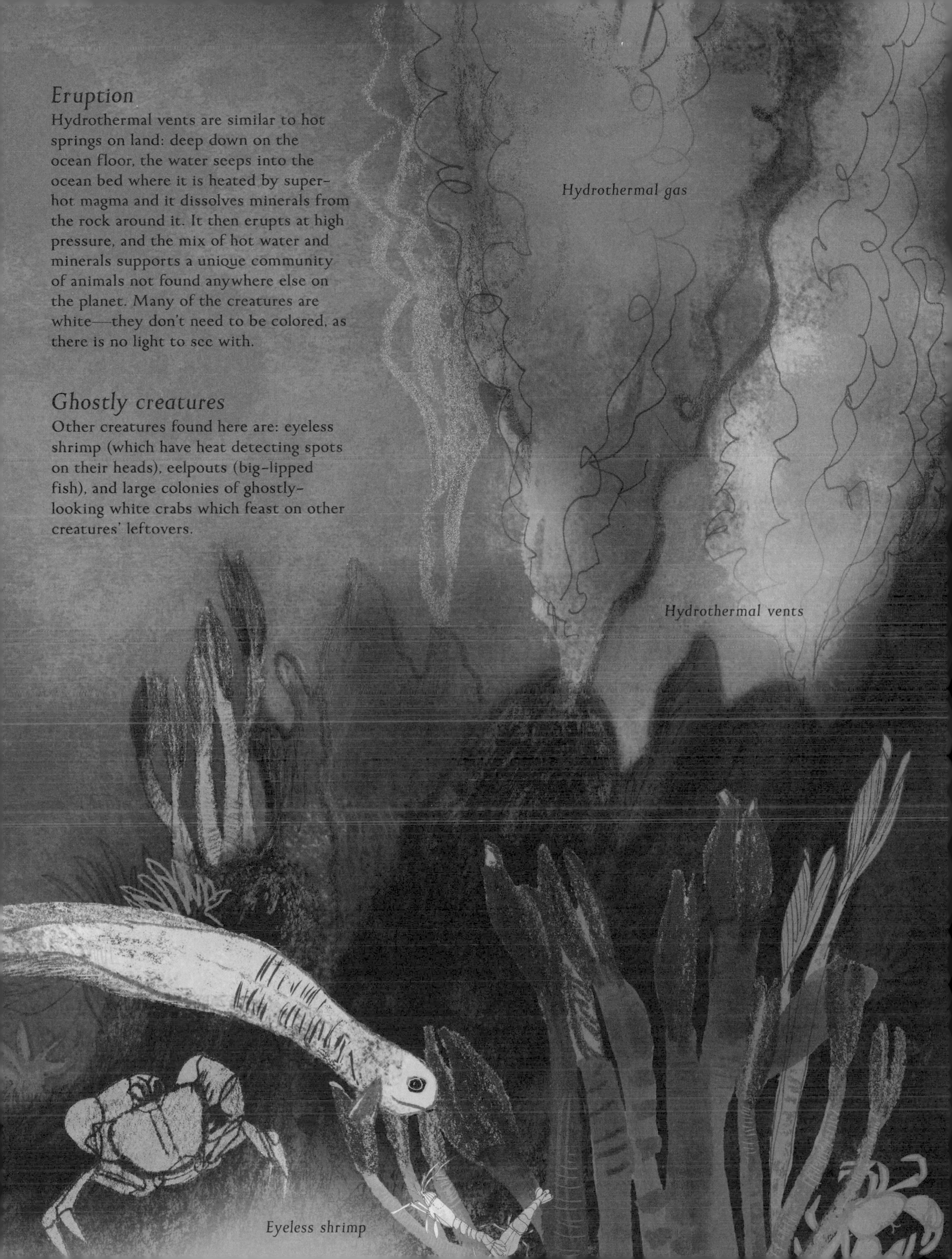

Hydrothermal gas

Hydrothermal vents

Eyeless shrimp

Deep Ocean Monsters

AWAY from the hydrothermal vents, the deep seabed is mostly barren, and food is scarce. Carcasses of dead marine creatures fall to the depths and attract grotesque-looking scavengers.

Hagfish

These jawless, eel-like fish have an incredible way of defending themselves: they make huge amounts of slime, which cover the gills or mouth of their attacker. Scientists have found that threads of this goo are more than one hundred times thinner than human hair and are five times stronger than steel.

Hagfish

Deep-sea coral

Half of all known coral species live in waters that are deep, dark, and cold—unlike the colorful coral reefs in tropical water. Deep-sea coral reefs are abundant in marine life, filtering food from the surrounding water. One deep-sea coral colony off Hawaii is over 4,000 years old: that's older than the Pyramids of Egypt!

Deep living fish

One of the deepest living fish recorded is the cusk eel, which was found at a depth of over 5 miles. So far, in water deeper than this, scientists have mostly found invertebrates such as shrimp-like crustaceans, sea cucumbers, and jellyfish.

Blobfish live at depths of up to 3,900 feet. They look like a blob of jelly, and they have been voted the world's ugliest animal!

Goblin shark

Goblin shark

Not much is known about this deep-sea dweller but, incredibly, you can see through the skin of this shark. It looks pink, but it's actually translucent: the pink color is caused by blood vessels beneath the skin.

Cusk eel

Blobfish

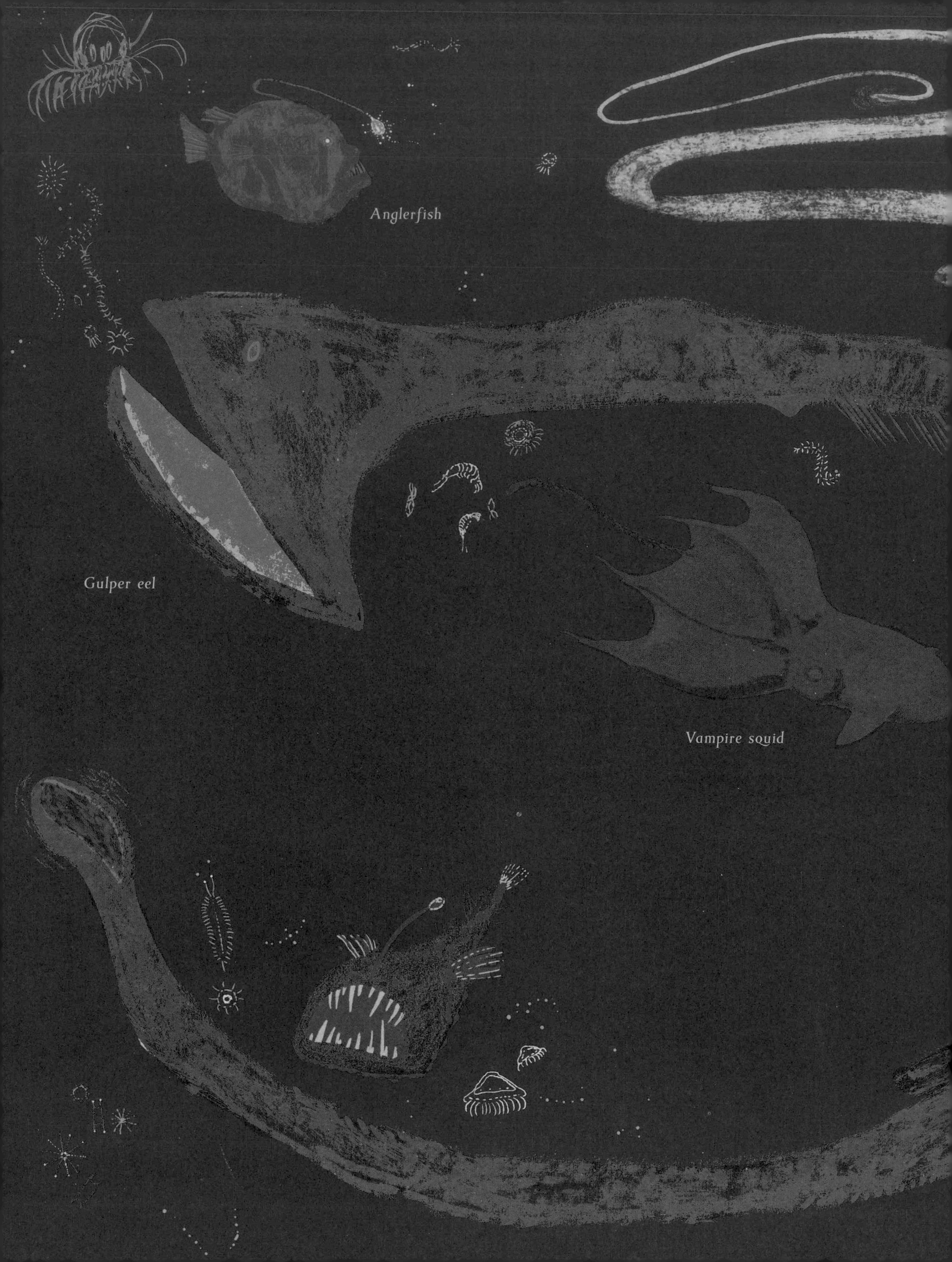

Anglerfish

Gulper eel

Vampire squid

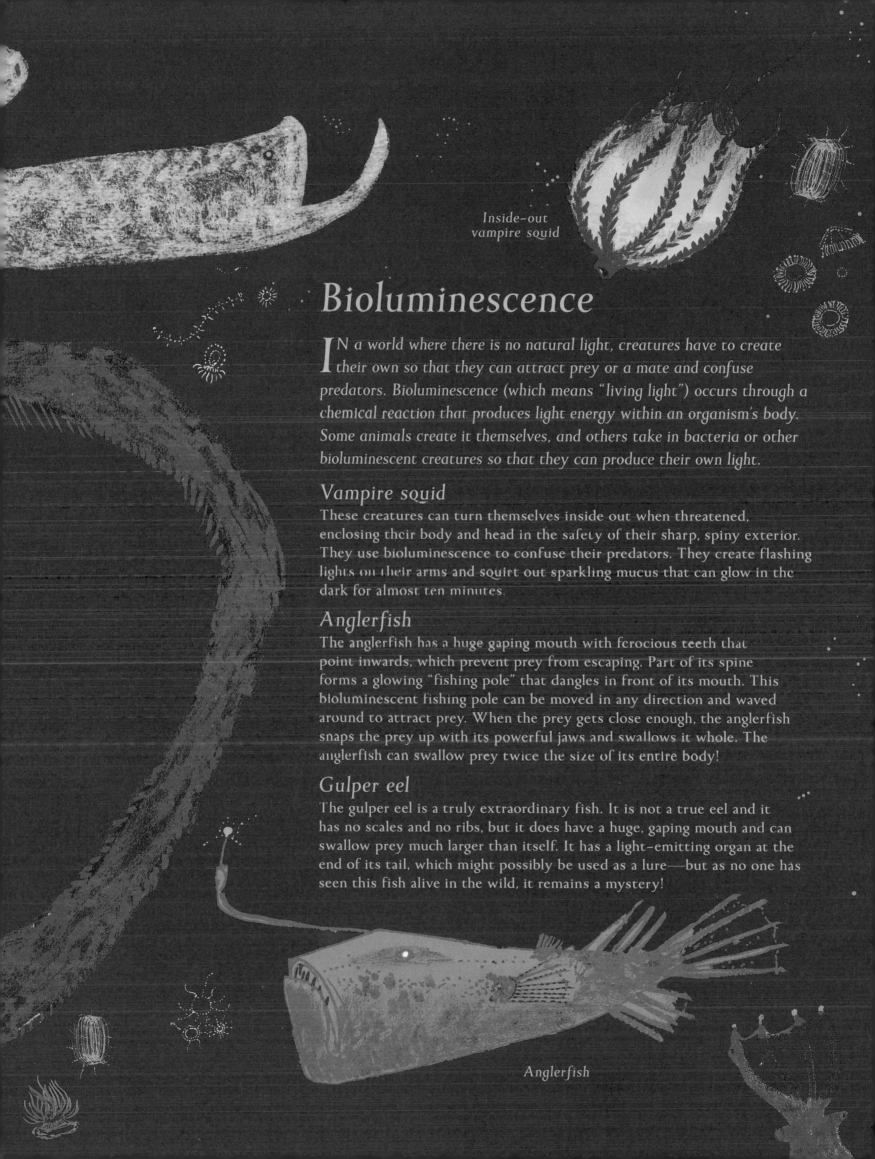

Inside-out
vampire squid

Bioluminescence

IN a world where there is no natural light, creatures have to create their own so that they can attract prey or a mate and confuse predators. Bioluminescence (which means "living light") occurs through a chemical reaction that produces light energy within an organism's body. Some animals create it themselves, and others take in bacteria or other bioluminescent creatures so that they can produce their own light.

Vampire squid

These creatures can turn themselves inside out when threatened, enclosing their body and head in the safety of their sharp, spiny exterior. They use bioluminescence to confuse their predators. They create flashing lights on their arms and squirt out sparkling mucus that can glow in the dark for almost ten minutes.

Anglerfish

The anglerfish has a huge gaping mouth with ferocious teeth that point inwards, which prevent prey from escaping. Part of its spine forms a glowing "fishing pole" that dangles in front of its mouth. This bioluminescent fishing pole can be moved in any direction and waved around to attract prey. When the prey gets close enough, the anglerfish snaps the prey up with its powerful jaws and swallows it whole. The anglerfish can swallow prey twice the size of its entire body!

Gulper eel

The gulper eel is a truly extraordinary fish. It is not a true eel and it has no scales and no ribs, but it does have a huge, gaping mouth and can swallow prey much larger than itself. It has a light-emitting organ at the end of its tail, which might possibly be used as a lure—but as no one has seen this fish alive in the wild, it remains a mystery!

Anglerfish

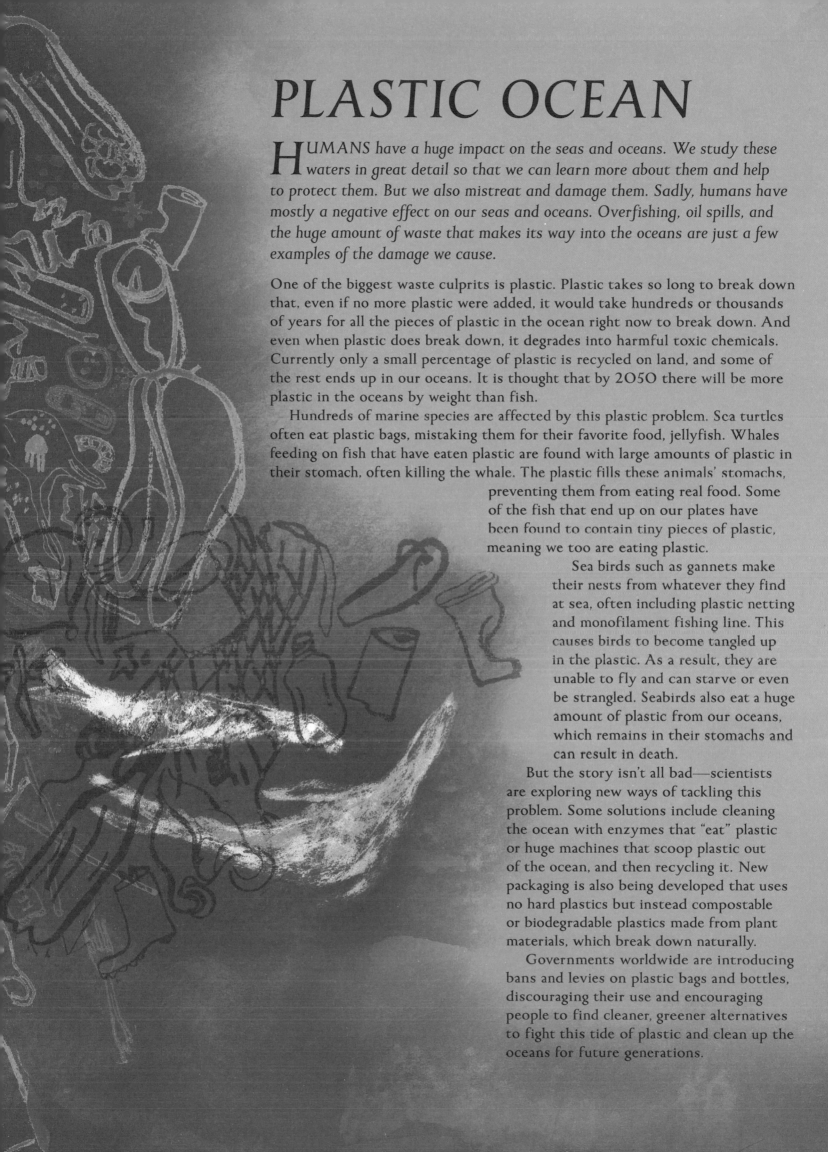

PLASTIC OCEAN

HUMANS *have a huge impact on the seas and oceans. We study these waters in great detail so that we can learn more about them and help to protect them. But we also mistreat and damage them. Sadly, humans have mostly a negative effect on our seas and oceans. Overfishing, oil spills, and the huge amount of waste that makes its way into the oceans are just a few examples of the damage we cause.*

One of the biggest waste culprits is plastic. Plastic takes so long to break down that, even if no more plastic were added, it would take hundreds or thousands of years for all the pieces of plastic in the ocean right now to break down. And even when plastic does break down, it degrades into harmful toxic chemicals. Currently only a small percentage of plastic is recycled on land, and some of the rest ends up in our oceans. It is thought that by 2050 there will be more plastic in the oceans by weight than fish.

Hundreds of marine species are affected by this plastic problem. Sea turtles often eat plastic bags, mistaking them for their favorite food, jellyfish. Whales feeding on fish that have eaten plastic are found with large amounts of plastic in their stomach, often killing the whale. The plastic fills these animals' stomachs, preventing them from eating real food. Some of the fish that end up on our plates have been found to contain tiny pieces of plastic, meaning we too are eating plastic.

Sea birds such as gannets make their nests from whatever they find at sea, often including plastic netting and monofilament fishing line. This causes birds to become tangled up in the plastic. As a result, they are unable to fly and can starve or even be strangled. Seabirds also eat a huge amount of plastic from our oceans, which remains in their stomachs and can result in death.

But the story isn't all bad—scientists are exploring new ways of tackling this problem. Some solutions include cleaning the ocean with enzymes that "eat" plastic or huge machines that scoop plastic out of the ocean, and then recycling it. New packaging is also being developed that uses no hard plastics but instead compostable or biodegradable plastics made from plant materials, which break down naturally.

Governments worldwide are introducing bans and levies on plastic bags and bottles, discouraging their use and encouraging people to find cleaner, greener alternatives to fight this tide of plastic and clean up the oceans for future generations.

BLOOMSBURY CHILDREN'S BOOKS
Bloomsbury Publishing Inc., part of Bloomsbury Publishing Plc
1385 Broadway, New York, NY 10018

First published in Great Britain as *The Sea* in April 2019 by Bloomsbury Publishing Plc
Published in the United States of America in February 2020 by Bloomsbury Children's Books

Library of Congress Cataloging-in-Publication Data
available upon request
ISBN 978-1-5476-0335-0 (hardcover)
ISBN 978-1-5476-0336-7 (e-book) • ISBN 978-1-5476-0341-1 (e-PDF)

Printed and bound in China by Leo Paper Products, Heshan, Guangdong
2 4 6 8 10 9 7 5 3 1

All papers used by Bloomsbury Publishing Plc are natural, recyclable products
made from wood grown in well-managed forests. The manufacturing processes
conform to the environmental regulations of the country of origin.

To find out more about our authors and books visit www.bloomsbury.com and sign up for our newsletters.